Watch Plants Grow!

WATCH APPLE TREES GROW

By Mary Ann Hoffman

Gareth Stevens
Publishing

Please visit our Web site, www.garethstevens.com. For a free color catalog of all our high-quality books, call toll free 1-800-542-2595 or fax 1-877-542-2596.

Library of Congress Cataloging-in-Publication Data

Hoffman, Mary Ann
Watch apple trees grow / Mary Ann Hoffman.
   p. cm. — (Watch plants grow!)
ISBN 978-1-4339-4817-6 (pbk.)
ISBN 978-1-4339-4818-3 (6-pack)
ISBN 978-1-4339-4816-9 (library binding)
1. Apples—Growth—Juvenile literature. 2. Apples—Development—Juvenile literature. I. Title.
QK495.M78M365 2011
634'.11—dc22

                          2010038514

First Edition

Published in 2011 by
Gareth Stevens Publishing
111 East 14th Street, Suite 349
New York, NY 10003

Editor: Kristen Rajczak
Designer: Haley W. Harasymiw

Photo credits: Cover, pp. 1, 3, 5, 9, 11, 15, 21, 23 Shutterstock.com; p. 7 Alistair Berg/Digital Vision/Getty Images; p. 13 (left) © Nigel Cattlin/Holt Studios/Photo Researchers, Inc.; p. 13 (right) © Maryann Frazier/Photo Researchers, Inc.; p. 17 Patrick Reddy/America 24-7/Getty Images p. 19 Ann Cutting/Botanica/Getty Images.

Printed in the United States of America

CPSIA compliance information: Batch #CW11GS: For further information contact Gareth Stevens, New York, New York at 1-800-542-2595.

WATCH
APPLE TREES
GROW

Apple trees grow from seeds.

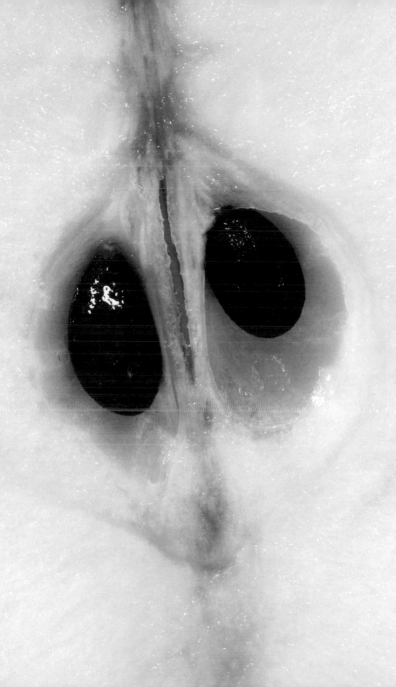

5

Plant seeds and watch them grow.

Sprouts grow from
the seeds.

Apple trees grow from the sprouts.

The apple trees grow buds. The buds open into flowers.

13

Bees fly from flower to flower. They help make apples grow.

The flowers fall off. You can see small apples.

17

The small apples are green. Some turn yellow as they grow. Some turn red.

19

Farmers pick the apples.
We buy apples at the store.

21

Apples are good to eat. Apples keep your teeth clean.

Words to Know

bud

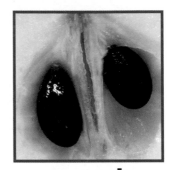

seeds

sprout